DEVELOPING TEACHING

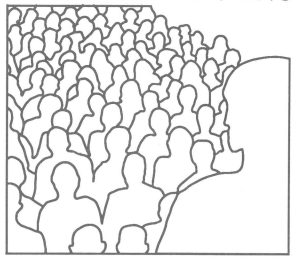

TEACHING MORE
STUDENTS

4
ASSESSING
MORE STUDENTS

Graham Gibbs

Design Team:
Alan Jenkins, Gina Wisker

Consultant Team:
Gina Wisker, Chris Rust,
David McAndrew, Alan Jenkins,
David Jaques, Trevor Habeshaw,
Graham Gibbs, Bob Farmer,
Diana Eastcott, Sally Brown,
Elizabeth Beaty, David Baume

The TEACHING MORE STUDENTS Project

The aim of the project is to offer lecturers and course leaders support in facing the challenge of increased student numbers and larger classes. It will be difficult to maintain quality in learning if course design, teaching and assessment methods remain unchanged. To support change, the project will deliver about 100 training workshops in Polytechnics and Colleges throughout England to about 3,000 academic staff. The workshops will be delivered in most institutions during 1992.

The workshops will be tailored to meet the needs of each institution, based on the following workshop modules:

1   Teaching more students: problems and strategic options
2   Lecturing to more students
3   Discussion with more students
4   Assessing more students
5   Independent learning with more students
6   Course design for teaching more students

The workshops will support lecturers by:

*   identifying the nature of teaching and learning problems encountered with increasing student numbers
*   offering a range of laternative strategies and methods, based on best practice, which can be used to address these problems
*   assisting lectures to select the most appropriate methods according to contexts, and to plantheir implementation
*   providing resource material to support follow-up work

The project will be delivered by a team of experienced educational development consultants from eight Polytechnics and Colleges, managed by the Oxford Centre for Staff Development under the direction of Graham Gibbs. The impact of the workshops on participants' teaching and institutions will be evaluated.

For further information contact:
The Oxford Centre for Staff and Learning Development
Oxford Brookes University
Gypsy Lane Campus
Oxford OX3 0BP
Tel 01865 484610 Fax 01865 484622

The TEACHING MORE STUDENTS Project
is funded by the Polytechnics and Colleges Funding Council

Contents

Workshop aims

By the end of the workshop participants will have:

- identified the main problems they and their students face where more students must be assessed;

- examined strategic options and specific assessment methods for addressing these problems;

- identified the most promising methods for their own contexts;

- had an opportunity to re-design the methods of assessment for one course for which they are responsible.

1   Students' and lecturers' experience of assessment

Students' experience...

"I didn't really know what I was supposed to be doing half the time, but I couldn't ever find the lecturer to ask. They never seem to be in their offices, or when they are they're busy."

"By the time you've got your essay back it's really just water under the bridge. You've moved on to something else and you couldn't really care less what they've written on it. It was about five weeks later last time."

"I've never done one of these reports before and I'm really not sure how to do it. The seminars are too big and too busy to ask and you can't ask in lectures."

"There must have been 30 of us in the library all chasing the articles for the same assignment to be handed in on the same day. How are you supposed to 'read around' and 'demonstrate familiarity with the literature' when the stuff is all out or hidden?"

"I got a lousy mark for the first one but I couldn't see why. There were just ticks and crosses and exclamation marks on it and a mark at the end. We've been given the next assignment and I can see I'm going to get a lousy mark again."

"I think there used to be regular coursework but it's all at the end now so we don't really have to do anything till the last few weeks."

Lecturers' experience...

"At the end of last term a colleague said 'All I have left to do is record all the marks' and I was at that stage too, but I also knew that simply writing down and checking all the marks for six assignments for 350 students took two long, boring days."

"We used to set and mark a lab report each week on each of the laboratory-based courses. If we did that now we'd be buried. You are talking about 30 hours a week marking on each module. There wouldn't be time to sleep."

"I'm worried that the students just don't get enough practice writing. It's not good enough just reverting to unseen exams at the end of the year because we then expect them to be able to write. How are they supposed to learn?"

"We pride ourselves on setting substantial programming projects and then going through them extremely carefully. It takes me about an hour and a half to mark one properly. You just can't spot things like elegance at a glance. We've now got 120 students on the course. That's four weeks' solid work doing nothing else but marking. Are we going to have to lower our standards?"

Assessment problems for students

As student enrolment on courses increases, the total amount of lecturer time spent on assessment can exceed the total amount of time spent teaching. Assessment practices which were manageable with fewer students become unsustainable as the sheer volume of marking increases. If lecturers bow under the pressure but do not change the nature of assessment then all assessed assignments tend to become fewer, shorter and less frequent, with more delayed, and superficial, feedback to students.

This leads to students getting less practice at writing, solving problems and undertaking the tasks involved in the assignments. This can be evident in poorer preparation for exams.

The proportion of the syllabus which is sampled by the assessment is reduced, leading to lower reliability, and a greater element of chance for students in terms of whether assessment concerns topics they happen to like, understand or have spent time on. It also encourages "selective negligence": students choose which parts of the course to ignore, knowing that only some parts will be assessed. As a result students put in fewer learning hours, studying less of the course in depth.

In the absence of frequent personal contact between tutor and student, motivation is generated through the assessment system. When the assessment system is wound down, motivation then drops. Students tend to work more sporadically, picking up only when assignments are due, and losing momentum in their studies.

As assessed coursework becomes less frequent, so a greater proportion of students' final degree classification hangs on each assignment. At the same time students have less guidance and less practice. The result is greater anxiety.

Where assessed work is closely related to teaching, as with laboratory reports in science and technology and problems in mathematics, students may take the laboratory sessions and problem classes less seriously, and even fail to attend them, when assessment is less frequent.

As the opportunity to obtain detailed guidance from tutors declines so students produce work of poorer quality and out of line with what is expected. This can itself generate extra demands on tutors to give appropriate feedback.

As marking loads increase, students receive less feedback on each piece of work. As the tutor may not know the students, this feedback may be impersonal and less well targetted than it could be. As the students may not know the marker, the feedback may not be interpreted appropriately and is likely to have less impact. As the time between submitting an assignment and getting it back with marks and comments lengthens, so students pay less and less attention to the feedback. There will be less opportunity to discuss the feedback with a tutor either in order to understand it or to identify how to improve. If the tutor who marks the work is part-time or brought in from another course to help out with the marking load, there may be no opportunity for discussion at all.

In the absence of regular feedback students lose a sense of how they are doing and what they should be paying attention to. Their efforts may be misdirected. They may gain an inaccurate impression of their performance, leading to either anxiety or complacency. Students are more likely to be tripped up by infrequent assessment and unexpected failure is more likely. Tutors will have little information on which students are struggling and will not be able to intervene before it is too late.

All these problems are the direct result of increasing student marking and loads generated by more students, which inevitably lead to a reduction in assessed work. The assessment strategies identified below offer ways of limiting or avoiding these problems.

2 Current assessment methods

In order to evaluate the potential of the strategies and ideas outlined below it may be helpful to have a particular course in mind where student numbers cause problems with the assessment. Completing this questionnaire will clarify the context and identify the crucial issues to be addressed in any re-design of the assessment.

---

1 How is the course assessed at present?
(How are marks arrived at and how are students given feedback on their progress?)

---

2 How long (in hours) does this assessment take you?
(a) to prepare the assessment tasks for the course (e.g. drafting exam questions);

(b) to provide guidance to students on the assessment tasks, in class or in tutorials;

(c) to mark and give feedback to students and to collate the assessment marks for the whole course.

---

3 Assuming a 50% increase in students next year, how much more time would the assessment take, using the same methods?

---

4 What are the problems for students, with regard to assessment, on this course?

3 Assessment strategies

The strategies outlined here are explained in detail in the pages that follow, together with examples. Reading these outlines should help you to make a provisional judgement about which are most appropriate to you.

3.1 Front-ending assessment

This involves more careful preparation of assignments, briefing of students and clarification of assessment criteria at the start so as to minimise problems that may occur later. Better preparation can enable students to work more independently, seeking less advice and avoiding misdirected effort, and can make for easier and quicker marking.

3.2 Doing it in class

This involves shifting to formal class sessions more of the time spent on advice to students on assignment tasks, and perhaps the assessment itself.

3.3 Self- and peer-assessment

This involves passing over to students part of the tutor's role, so that students themselves carry out many more of the tasks of assessment and feedback.

3.4 Assessing students as groups

This involves creating tasks which require students to work in small groups and then assessing them as groups. For the teacher, this reduces the number of pieces of work that have to be assessed and the amount of time spent supervising work on assignments.

3.5 Mechanising assessment

This involves automating and standardising assessment; it can include objective assessment, using computer technology, and "tick box" marking and feedback forms.

3.6 Cutting down on assessment and feedback

This involves tough decisions concerning priorities and being selective about what to assess and what to provide feedback on, in relation to course objectives. It may involve setting fewer assignments but designing them more carefully, and giving less, but more focussed, feedback. Reducing assessment and feedback involves a more strategic approach than simply cutting out a proportion of all assignments or cutting down on marking time or volume of feedback.

3.1   Front-ending assessment

Front-ending assessment means putting more of your time and energy into the assessment system well before the course starts or before students undertake assignments. This recognises the importance of assessment in shaping what students learn. As a way of coping with more students it ensures that students are well aware of what is expected of them and can then work more independently and yet produce quality work. By avoiding misdirected work it also saves marking time.

Almost whichever other strategy you also adopt, front-ending is vital with large classes.

The examples of front-ending illustrated below are:

3.1.1 Full instructions for assignments
3.1.2 Clarifying criteria
  • **First-class answer**
  • **Written criteria**
3.1.3 Briefing using criteria

3.1.1   Full instructions for assignments

Full written instructions should be designed to anticipate all the things which students do wrong and misunderstand about the purpose and content of assignments. They are particularly important on modular courses, where assumptions about, for example, how to write an essay, vary from subject to subject. The longer and more complex the assignment, for example final-year dissertation or project work, the more useful are full instructions, and the more of the tutor's time will be saved.

As an example, here is part of five pages of instructions on how to write up a practical report for a Psychology laboratory course with about 100 students.

Writing up the method section

If you are writing up an experiment or study begin the method section by describing the general features of the experimental approach, stating the independent and dependent variables and the units of measurement. The independent variable is that which is manipulated by the experimenter, whereas the dependent variable is that which is measured. If you are reporting a study, where there are neither independent nor dependent variables, a brief description of the design of the study should be included.

This section is then broken down under several sub-headings.

(a) Subjects. State the total number of subjects used in the study. Then give the number of females and males. Where possible give the age range, average age and the source of the sample. For example, "The sample consisted of 80

Polytechnic students enrolled on The Individual and Society module. There were 35 males and 45 females.*

In reporting psychological findings it is important to specify your subjects as precisely as possible since individual differences in performance are likely to produce important differences in results.

(b) Materials. Description and/or diagrams of materials used and apparatus arrangements.

In most cases it is necessary only to name the piece of apparatus used since descriptions are available elsewhere, e.g. stopwatch, Eysenck Personality Inventory. Copies of questionnaires may be included in the Appendix to your report, although this is not strictly necessary. If, however, the equipment or the questionnaire have been designed specially for this study, a full description is required.

(c) Procedure. Detailed description of what happened during the experiment or study. Report verbatim the instructions which were given to the subjects. The guiding principle here is that your description of procedure should be sufficiently detailed to allow another scientist to repeat your experiment in exactly the same way as you performed it. Discuss the provisions made to isolate and control all the relevant variables which may have influenced the results, e.g. practice, fatigue.

This section should conclude with an outline of how the scores were collected and how the results were scored or coded.

3.1.2 Clarifying criteria

The criteria used by tutors in assessing student work are often effectively secret; they are not publicly acknowledged by the tutor, discussed with colleagues or directly communicated to students. In small courses informal exchanges between teachers and students can clear up many of these uncertainties about criteria. With more students there is not enough time for these informal exchanges and, where there are a number of tutors teaching and assessing, students receive conflicting signals on what is required. Making your assessment criteria clear is a cost-effective way of briefing students. It can also speed marking and feedback (see 3.5 "Mechanising assessment").

First-class answer

In this strategy the tutor tells students, at the beginning of the course, what the difference would be between assignments which received different grades. This helps by clarifying what students should not be doing, as well as what they should be aiming at. Below are extracts from an example from a course called Britain's Changing Geography.

Describe what you consider to be the central changes to the economic and social geography of Britain since c1970. How would you account for these changes?

First class

Assess the <u>central</u> <u>changes</u> to the <u>economic</u> <u>and</u> <u>social</u> <u>geography</u> of Britain since <u>1970</u> - considering carefully what is meant by the key words underlined and emphasising those changes since 1970. Identify and discuss the <u>key</u> <u>factors</u> or <u>processes</u> that explain why these changes have occurred, carefully demonstrating the link between process and geographic change. Throughout the essay use empirical detail to support your argument. The answer will indicate controversies in the literature that describe and explain these changes, etc.

Upper second class

Describe the central <u>changes</u> to the <u>economic and social</u> geography of Britain since <u>1970</u> - recognising the importance of the key words underlined. Use empirical detail/ evidence to support your argument. Do not consider it essential to bring out controversies in the literature on either the nature of the changes or their causes, or to adopt a well-supported argument of your own. Use only material covered in class or in compulsory reading.

Lower second class

Describe some of the recent changes to the human geography of Britain. Do not be too precise in identifying the changes or in giving evidence that supports your argument. Loosely relate those changes to some of the factors or processes that may have caused them. It is not necessary to emphasise the complexity of or uncertainty about what has occurred, or the reasons for the apparent changes. Stick closely to material given to you in class and some of the compulsory reading - do not go beyond that information. It is not important to draw out how different academics (particularly geographers) interpret the evidence nor to advance a clear argument of your own.

Third class

Write an essay on recent changes to the geography of Britain. Make vague unsubstantiated statements about the changes. Throw in now and then some sense that these changes are the result of some factors or processes, but generally do not link clearly the changes and processes. Give very little evidence for your assertions and restrict that evidence to what you learnt in class and just some of the compulsory reading. Either construct a simple argument that has little or no logic and supporting evidence or throw in a variety of conflicting and poorly thought-out ideas.

Fail

Write down almost anything you can think of about Britain's geography but do not attempt to structure it in any way. Jump around between discussing the changes and the causes, not letting your reader understand the difference between them - suggesting that you do not understand them yourself. Ensure that there is little structure to a well-nigh illegible answer. Make unsupported statements and/or, where any evidence is offered, stick to what you vaguely remember from one or two of the classes you attended. Leave the reader doubting whether you have learnt anything from the course.

Written criteria

In providing written criteria, the tutor tries to identify as clearly as possible to students, and to fellow markers, the criteria to be used in assessing this specific assignment. You may even want to specify the percentage of marks allocated to each section.

Here is how one group of Education tutors specified to students what they would be looking for in a dissertation:

Dissertation Criteria

(a) Clear statement of the focus/area/topic/problem/hypothesis.

(b) Substantive review of the relevant literature. Good relation of theory and literature to the actual research being undertaken, including justification of research topic/setting(s)/programme.

(c) Choice of appropriate research method(s), setting(s) and programme.

(d) Clear description of the research method(s), setting(s) and programme.

(e) Appropriate and sufficient collection and clear presentation of data.

(f) Thoroughness of critical analysis and evaluation of the research, with clear and detailed reference to data and to literature, appropriate theories and explanations, and some appraisal of validity and value.

(g) Sensitivity to problems and processes of research undertaken, e.g. ethics, communication, negotiation, collaboration, dissemination.

(h) Substantial conclusion, raising key issues and points, with suggestions for future research/practice as appropriate.

(i) Full, accurate bibliography. Appendices as appropriate.

3.1.3 Briefing using criteria

It is not always realistic to use all criteria every time an assignment is set. It is possible to focus students' attention on a sub-set and give marks and feedback only in relation to that sub-set. While students are learning to undertake assignments in an appropriate way it may be very helpful not to expect too wide a range of expertise at once. This also saves time when marking. The essay briefing sheet reproduced below illustrates this approach. English Literature students can be briefed to pay attention to any sub-set of the criteria listed, for example knowledge of the author and the social and historical context of the text, or essay-writing and use of critical theory.

Essay Briefing and Marking Sheet

Criteria	Advice	Max mark	Your mark	Comments
Knowledge of text, author, genre, historical and social context				
Essay Structure, use of quotations and other sources				
Personal Response to text, viewpoint and creativity				
Critical theory Understanding and use of critical methods				
Language Commentary on use of language				
Other criteria				

3.2   Doing it in class

Assessing more students can result in tutors spending much time in their offices seeing individual students to discuss how to proceed on an assignment or giving feedback on an assigned task. Students may have difficulty finding the tutor in without a queue at the door.

Tutors also can spend hours at home and in their offices marking assignments and exams. It is possible to use class time to give students help on how to proceed with an assignment. It is also possible to create assessment tasks that can be carried out and marked in class.

Specific examples of this strategy include:

3.2.1 Providing class time to discuss assignments
3.2.2 Setting assignments which can be marked in class
- **Presentations**
- **Posters**
- **Multiple choice questions and problems**

3.2.3 Setting assignments which can be undertaken in class

3.2.1   Providing class time to discuss assignments

Even if you have carefully specified what students should do and the criteria to be used in allocating marks (see 3.1 "Front-ending assessment") there may still be students who are uncertain what is required. Many students leave assignment tasks until the last minute and then come pounding on your door for advice. The following is an account of how one tutor handled the problem:

Class discussion of an assignment with 120 students

Step 1 The course guide clearly specified the assessment task and also stated that it would be discussed in class on a particular date.

Step 2 In the preceding class session the tutor referred students to that part of the course guide and told them she wanted them each to write three queries on how to complete the assignment satisfactorily, and bring their queries to the next class.

Step 3 In the class scheduled for the discussion, the students were asked to form groups of four to six and come up with three queries on the assignment which they wanted the tutor to answer. They were to write the names of the group members and their three queries on a sheet of paper and hand it to their tutor.

Step 4 While students were busy working in class on an assigned task the tutor skimmed through the queries and identified those she considered central. She then answered them in a brief presentation and made clear that from then on the students were on their own, though of course they could help each other.

3.2.2 Setting assignments which can be marked in class

This strategy cuts down the marking outside class contact time. For students, it means they get rapid feedback on what they have done. Examples of this strategy include assessing presentations in class (such as seminar presentations), posters, multiple choice questions and problems.

Presentations

Students individually or in small groups are given a task to complete outside class and demonstrate what they have learnt through a presentation. This is a method applicable to most discursive subjects and is especially appropriate for languages, dance, drama and visual subjects. The tutor can assess the presentation there and then. It is important to specify criteria in order to orientate the students appropriately and standardise the tutor's marking. Students can get involved in assessing their peers' and/or their own presentations (see 3.3 "Self- and peer-assessment").

Posters

Students individually or in small groups are given a task to complete (probably, but not necessarily, outside class) and demonstrate what they have learnt through a poster. The class session is similar to the poster sessions which are now a feature of many academic conferences. Students can examine and discuss the findings displayed on the posters. Again criteria for assessing posters are important so that there is not an excessive attention to flashy graphics to the exclusion of content. (Jenkins and Pepper, 1988). Part of the session is devoted to the teacher or the students assessing the posters (see Booklet 3: *Discussion with More Students* for an explanation of poster sessions). Poster sessions can work very well for laboratory work because students seldom see the work others have done.

Although presentations may be public, assessment need not be. If assessment is in public it is important to be particularly sensitive to students' feelings on the marks and feedback they receive. One basic rule here is always to start by stating what is good about what has been produced.

Reference

Jenkins, A. and Pepper, D. M. (1988), *Developing Group Work and Communication Skills: A Manual for Teachers in Higher Education*. Birmingham: Standing Conference on Educational Development.

Multiple choice questions and problems

Simple objective tests (see 3.5 "Mechanising assessment") and problems can be set and marked by students in class. For feedback purposes students can mark their own work and you can give a brief presentation of tutorial comments for each question and explain why the incorrect answers are wrong. Given a set of answers, students can mark one another's work. It is a simple matter to sample 10% of tests to check that students are doing a good job (see 3.3 "Self- and peer-assessment").

3.2.3   Setting assignments which can be undertaken in class

Laboratory sessions often require students to write up long reports after the lab. These can take a considerable time for the teacher to mark - often more than the time spent teaching the laboratory session. In developing their scientific understanding it is often important for students to show their doubts and uncertainties, the approaches that did not work. Too often lab reports written up after the session smooth over these doubts. What is assessed is students' ability to cover up what they actually did in the lab.

As an alternative you can require the students to complete the laboratory report in class as they undertake the experiment, and hand it in as they leave. This can have the benefit of forcing students to give more attention to what they are doing in that session.

Instant lab reports tend to be much briefer and thus much quicker to mark and can be much more revealing about students' laboratory practice (Gibbs *et al.*, 1989; Gibbs and Jaques, 1990).

References

Gibbs, G., Habeshaw, S. and Habeshaw, T. (1989) *53 Interesting Ways to Assess your Students.* Bristol: Technical and Educational Services.

Gibbs, G. and Jaques, D. (1990), *Labs and Practicals.* Oxford: Educational Methods Unit, Oxford Polytechnic.

3.3   Self- and peer-assessment

Students can perform a variety of assessment tasks in ways which both save the tutor's time and bring educational benefits. Students benefit from reviewing their own work before submitting it. They can usefully comment on each other's work so as to allow re-drafting before submission. Students are in a good position to assess seminar presentations and seminar contributions and are in the best position to contribute to assessment of relative contributions to group work (see 3.4 "Assessing students as groups"). Students are also capable of assessing each other's work and producing sufficiently reliable marks, given appropriate guidance.

The methods described below would not all be suitable for instant implementation. Students need to be introduced to self-assessment gradually, gaining experience before being asked to do anything too sophisticated. They need to develop in their judgement, and this takes time and practice. They need to be convinced of the value, and validity, of self-assessment. For this reason it is safer to start with self- and peer-assessment for the purpose of feedback rather than to get involved straight away with marking which counts towards a final qualification. Students should always have an opportunity to calibrate their judgements and marks against those of the tutor before their own marks are taken into account. It is also sensible to provide your own criteria for early self-assessment ventures before allowing students to use their own criteria.

The examples of self- and peer-assessment described here are:

3.3.1 Essay self-assessment forms
3.3.2 Self- and peer-assessment of seminar presentations
3.3.3 Self- and peer-assessment of seminar contributions
3.3.4 Self- and peer-assessment using a model answer

3.3.1 Essay self-assessment forms

The first self-assessment form below (taken from Jenkins and Pepper, 1988) is completed by students and attached to their essays when they submit them. They are required to give their judgement of how they have performed in terms of the stated criteria (which are listed following the form). Instead of commenting freely, students can be asked to respond to questions such as:

- What are the best features of this piece of work?
- How could this piece of work be improved?
- What would you have to do to get one grade higher than the grade you are going to get?
- What would you most like comments on?
- Which aspects of your report are you most confident about, and why?
- Which aspects of your report are you least confident about, and why?

Reference

Jenkins, A. and Pepper, D. M. (1988), *Developing Group Work and Communication Skills: A Manual for Teachers in Higher Education*. Birmingham: Standing Conference on Educational Development.

Essay Self-Assessment Form

Using the standards and criteria outlined in the course guide, allocate a grade to your essay and then write (below) a justification of the grade in terms of those criteria. You must give *detailed reasons* for why (and where) you think the essay has succeeded and failed. *A few words will not do.*

NAME   ....

ASSIGNMENT TITLE   ....

SELF-ASSESSMENT GRADE AWARDED   ....

JUSTIFICATION:

PARTICULAR PROBLEMS YOU ENCOUNTERED

TUTOR'S COMMENT AND GRADE

Essay Self-Assessment Criteria

1   Is the essay a reasoned argument in which the writer endeavours to *persuade* a sceptical reader of the justifiability of the line of argument adopted?

2   Is the argument *clear*? Is each part of it *clear*? Is it easy to understand and does it make sense? Is it presented *logically*?

3   Arising out of this, is there a *development* in reasoning, in which the clarity and significance of one point stems from the existence of a previous point? To help such development and make clear to the reader what course the argument will take:

   (i) considerable *planning* is necessary. (When you plan an essay, do not stop the process when you have arrived at a first plan. Go on to try to think of a second and subsequent ways of achieving your objective: the first way is not always the best - it frequently is not even the most obvious way!)

   (ii) sub-heads are necessary. These should not necessarily be one-word tel-egraphic sub-heads: they should express concisely what is to be found in the section following them. Do not get the wrong ideas about sub-heads: they do <u>not</u> "break up" an essay - on the contrary, they make it flow and integrate the elements of the argument in the reader's mind. They make for vastly greater clarity. Most published academic work uses them, so do most newspapers; in both, communication is important. *Use sub-heads.*

4   Is there an initial statement of the stance that is to be adopted? This statement may involve comment on how a question is to be interpreted, what kind of information is pertinent and why it is pertinent. *Beware*- an initial statement does not involve *waffle* - waffle is needless and often meaningless material. Do not waste time and valuable space writing it.

5   Arising from this, is all the material *relevant*? Is the relevance *explained*? You must keep reminding the reader *why* the point you are making is significant and how it relates (a) to the sub-head, (b) possibly to the wider theme. You should also ask yourself *how relevant* your material is. Only if it has "first-order" relevance will you wish to put it in the main body of the text. If its relevance is of second order, put it into a footnote. If it is third-order, leave it out altogether.

6   Are opinions and assertions (which are welcome) *evidenced* or *backed up* in some way, e.g. by reference to published work in the field, by data or by detailed argument? Such back-up material may often be put into footnotes and appendices, but it should be there.

7   Are *examples* of what you are referring to given at all possible times?

8   Does the essay stick to discussion and argument, rather than description? In essays in this course the reader generally wants to know more about *why* X says what he says. The latter can often be summarised in footnotes.

9   Is the essay repetitive? It should not be!

10 Is it generally clear, readable, correctly referenced and presented? Will it make the reader *want* to read it?

The English Literature self-assessment sheet below was designed to help students to recognise when they were overlooking crucial aspects of an essay. Students had been simply "telling the story" of a text instead of doing all the other things which are expected. By being required to review their own essays in this fairly mechanical way students started to supervise themselves, re-drafting work before submitting it and reducing the need for extensive tutor feedback.

Essay-Marking Criteria

Knowledge

Text	deep, thorough, detailed knowledge	☐	☐	☐	☐	☐	superficial knowledge
Author	wide knowledge used in analysis	☐	☐	☐	☐	☐	knowledge lacking or not used
Genre	wide knowledge used in analysis	☐	☐	☐	☐	☐	knowledge lacking or not used
Historical and social context	wide knowledge used in analysis	☐	☐	☐	☐	☐	knowledge lacking or not used

Essay

Structure	clear, logical structure	☐	☐	☐	☐	☐	confused list
Quotations	correct, purposeful use properly referenced	☐	☐	☐	☐	☐	references lacking or incorrect
Other sources	wide range, relevant properly referenced	☐	☐	☐	☐	☐	none or irrelevant
Grammar, spelling	correct	☐	☐	☐	☐	☐	many errors

Personal

Response to text	vivid, personal	☐	☐	☐	☐	☐	no response
Viewpoint	clearly expressed	☐	☐	☐	☐	☐	viewpoint lacking or unoriginal
Creativity	imaginative, surprising	☐	☐	☐	☐	☐	predictable

Critical theory

Understanding	clear grasp	☐	☐	☐	☐	☐	no grasp
Use of methods	wide range appropriately used	☐	☐	☐	☐	☐	range limited inappropriately used

3.3.2 Self- and peer-assessment of seminar presentations

Students can be required to assess their performance in an oral presentation, using free comments similar to those asked for on the essay self-assessment form above. Alternatively they can be given clear criteria (see Booklet 3: *Discussion with More Students*) or invited to devise their own criteria at the start of the course. The main impact of such self-assessment is to improve students' presentation performance and to reduce the need for detailed tutor feedback.

If you want to award marks for seminar presentations you can use student peer-assessment, employing the Seminar Assessment Criteria form in Booklet 3: *Discussion with More Students*. It is perfectly feasible for students to assess seminar presentations in an adequately rigorous way without a tutor being present at the seminar.

3.3.3 Self- and peer-assessment of seminar contributions

It is possible to use self-assessment to improve almost any aspect of students' studying. In the example below it is used to change the way students participate in seminars. It is also possible to get students to rate each other's contributions to seminar groups. In both cases the tutor can retain the final decision, but can rely to an extent on students' own assessments to save time.

Contribution to Seminar's Effectiveness: Self-Assessment Form

10% of the total course grade is an assessment of your contribution to the seminar's effectiveness. Consider how you have contributed to the seminars during the whole of the term. For each of the criteria listed below comment upon how you think you have performed. Note that what your tutor is looking for is self-critical awareness so do not exaggerate your strengths or your limitations. Finally, for your overall performance suggest a mark out of 10.

NAME ....

(A) ATTENDANCE AT AND PREPARATION FOR THE SEMINAR

(B) QUALITY OF YOUR CONTRIBUTION TO THE GROUP. TO WHAT EXTENT DID YOU SUPPLY INFORMATION AND IDEAS THAT WERE USEFUL TO THE GROUP?

(C) RECEPTIVENESS TO THE IDEAS OF OTHERS. TO WHAT EXTENT DID YOU ALLOW OTHERS TO CONTRIBUTE, AND LISTEN TO WHAT THEY HAD TO SAY?

(D) FACILITATING THE GROUP'S COHESION. TO WHAT EXTENT DID YOU ENCOURAGE OTHERS TO CONTRIBUTE?

YOUR SUGGESTED MARK OUT OF 10   ....

TUTOR'S MARK   ....

TUTOR'S COMMENTS

3.3.4 Self- and peer-assessment using model answers

In scientific and technical subjects it is often possible to specify "model" answers which can be used to standardise marking, particularly between different markers. It is relatively straightforward for students to use these model answers to assess each other's work. In the study described below students were involved in self- and peer-assessment in an Electrical Engineering examination.

This study investigated the limited notion of student self-marking with a third-year undergraduate class of over one hundred students studying electronic circuits at the University of New South Wales. Students were involved in assessing their own performance and that of one of their peers in a mid-semester examination.

As an alternative to the normal marking procedure for this examination, students received detailed model answers and commentaries with which they could compare their own solutions - or those of their peers - in the completed examination papers and thus allocate marks.

At the first class meeting after the examination each was randomly allocated the unnamed paper of one other student in the class. They marked this in their own time using the model answers and marking schedule.

They were required to indicate in detail on a marking sheet exactly where the other student had departed from the model solution and to award a score for each section on a scale provided. They returned the papers and marking sheets the following week and received their own examination script.

They then applied the same procedure to their own paper without knowing what marks might have already been awarded it by someone else. The self- and peer-generated marks for the examination were then compared and, if percentage marks were within 10% of each other then the student was awarded the self-mark. In cases of greater discrepancy than 10%, the paper was re-marked by a staff member. In order to discourage students colluding with each other to fix marks to maximise their grade (which had earlier been identified as a potential problem) other papers were sampled at random by staff.

A procedure for administering this scheme was evolved over four successive semesters to minimise staff time, to ensure equitable distribution of papers and to minimise collusion in mark-fixing. Student response was positive and staff reported that there was a considerable saving in staff marking time, even allowing for the increase in time in preparing model answers and organising the movement of papers. The saving was calculated to be greater the larger the number of students enrolled in the class.

This study also showed that it is possible to develop a self-marking procedure which is acceptable to both staff and students. The crucial condition is that the scheme be progressively modified to address at least some of the problems and deficiencies which inevitably occur when any scheme of this type is introduced.

Boud, D. (1986), *Implementing Student Self-Assessment*, Green Guide no. 5. Sydney: Higher Education Research and Development Society of Australasia, pp.6-7.

3.4   Assessing students as groups

There are many educationally valid reasons for getting students to co-operate in groups for part of their studies, and many practical ways to arrange this. These are explored particularly in Booklet 5: *Independent Learning with More Students*. This section is concerned only with the assessment of groups.

An important advantage for tutors of group work is that the number of pieces of work that have to be assessed is significantly reduced. For example, in a class of 100 students who are divided into groups of four for an assignment only 25 pieces of work have to be assessed. A group assignment may take a little longer to mark than an individual's assignment, but not four times as long. It is also possible, or even desirable, to involve students in some of the assessment, as they are in the best position to judge the relative contributions of individuals within groups.

The main objections to assessing groups are:

*   Individuals are awarded qualifications, not groups. Somehow marks need to be awarded to individuals.

*   If everyone in a group simply obtains the group's grade this encourages and allows back-sliding by some group members, who can get the group grade without doing any work or learning anything.

*   Outstanding students can be dragged down by poor or lazy colleagues and some mechanism needs to be introduced to compensate for this.

*   Group work tends to be of higher quality than individual work. This is fine as far as demonstrating the overall quality of a course, but causes problems in that the average scores of the whole class are raised above what might be considered appropriate.

*   Working in groups averages out differences between students and this produces a narrower spread of marks between groups than is normal between individuals.

The methods described below (drawn from Gibbs *et al.*, 1992) address some or all of these problems:

3.4.1 **Group mark**
3.4.2 **Divided group work and contracts**
3.4.3 **Divided group mark**
3.4.4 **Peer-assessment of contributions**
3.4.5 **Individual viva**
3.4.6 **Project exam questions**

Whichever methods are adopted the following guidelines may be useful:

- Do not make the groups too large. Groups of more than six are cumbersome and difficult to manage. They are also easy for lazy students to hide in. For short tasks, threes may be appropriate. For substantial projects, up to six can work well.

- Help students to work in groups - they will not find this a natural or easy thing to do.

- Explain the assessment system, including the criteria and ways for allocating marks, at the start. This will reassure individuals about the mechanisms built in to protect the hard-working and warn off individuals who were planning to have an easy ride.

- Form groups randomly. Allowing students to form their own groups results in friends getting together (and they are unlikely to form a disciplined or rigorous group who are prepared to be tough with each other) or the best students getting together (which leaves very poor groups who struggle).

- Do not leave students in the same group for too long. One term or one major project is likely to be quite enough. It is both fairer and more effective to change groups from time to time.

3.4.1 Group mark

Under some circumstances it is appropriate to give all members of a group the group mark, for example where it is important that students learn that the overall effectiveness of a group depends on the co-operativeness of its members. It may even be appropriate to allow students to select their own members, in order that they learn the importance of appropriate selection. However, there can be a high price to pay for such learning and a group mark is not often a sensible strategy.

3.4.2 Divided group work and contracts

If the assignment has a number of distinct components then individuals can be given, or can negotiate, responsibility for these components. The group members can draw up an agreement, or contract, specifying which components each group member is responsible for. You can either mark the components separately or, putting the responsibility back on the students, ask them to assess the extent to which members fulfilled their contracts and completed their components successfully. They can be allowed to moderate the tutor's group mark up or down 5% for each member.

This kind of divided group work can lead to parallel individual work rather than real group co-operation, so it is important to arrange for work to be divided up in a way which requires interdependence.

3.4.3 Divided group mark

If you have a group of six, and their project report or other assessed product has gained a mark of 50%, then you simply give the group 6 x 50 = 300 marks to divide between themselves as they see fit. The students are in the best position to know who deserves what mark. However, they may find it too difficult to decide, and "opt out", agreeing to give everyone the same mark despite obvious differences in contributions within the group. This is then their responsibility rather than yours and any unfairness is of their own making. However, you can avoid there being unequal contributions, and elicit different marks for group members. You can ask the group, at the start of the assignment, to discuss how they will divide up the marks at the end, and to specify in writing what criteria they will use. Students in the group will then be aware from the outset what the consequences will be of not pulling their weight, and they will make sure that they are seen to contribute fully. When you have marked and handed back the assignment you then ask the group to use their own criteria to divide up the marks. This tends to produce greater discrimination between group members and avoids some of the social awkwardness of peer-assessment.

3.4.4 Peer-assessment of contributions

You can direct students' efforts and establish criteria by specifying a number of aspects of the assignment which you want students to pay attention to. In the example below, the criteria highlight the successive stages of a Social Science enquiry. You mark the assignment and then ask the group to assess the relative contributions of each member to each of these aspects, allowing them to moderate individual marks up or down a little. The only rule is that the average of the moderated marks must be the same as your group mark: in other words they are not allowed all to mark each other up. You can specify any aspects or criteria you like, and might wish to specify different criteria for different assignments.

Peer-Assessment of Contributions to the Project Report					
Aspect of the project	**Relative contribution to the project**				
	below average		average		above average
Formulation of the problem	-2%	-1%	0%	+1%	+2%
Design of the study	-2%	-1%	0%	+1%	+2%
Collection of the data	-2%	-1%	0%	+1%	+2%
Analysis of the data	-2%	-1%	0%	+1%	+2%
Writing of theoretical section	-2%	-1%	0%	+1%	+2%
Presentation of results	-2%	-1%	0%	+1%	+2%
Tutor's group mark			....		
Sum of moderated marks (-12% to +12%)			....		
Individual mark			....		

3.4.5 Individual viva

It is possible to obtain a shrewd impression of the contribution of an individual to a group assignment in a brief viva. You have the assignment in front of you and ask questions such as "What was your contribution to this section?" and "Whose idea was this?". You could allow yourself the freedom to moderate students' marks up or down a maximum of 10% depending on the impression obtained in the viva. Again it is important that students know at the outset that they will be viva'd as this will change their behaviour in their group. Obviously vivas take time, but marking one substantial assignment and conducting a series of brief vivas can still be quicker than marking a series of assignments.

3.4.6 Project exam questions

A danger with group work is that if students are to be examined at a later date they may opt out of the group work in order to concentrate on revision. You can avoid this problem and obtain a mark for each individual within a group by making exam questions refer to the group assignment or project. Questions can take a variety of forms such as:

Q.   Describe how your group went about...

Q.   If your group had been asked to...instead of being asked to... how would you have gone about it?

Q.   Identify the strengths and weaknesses of your group's work, and explain how you would tackle a similar task differently next time.

Q.   Explain the concept of... with reference to your group project.

Q.   What methods can be used to...?. Select one of these methods to explain in detail, using your group project as an example.

Reference

Gibbs, G., Habeshaw, S. and Habeshaw, T. (1992), *53 Interesting Ways to Teach Large Classes.* Bristol: Technical and Educational Services.

3.5   Mechanising assessment

As student numbers increase, the main assessment problem for tutors is the amount of time marking takes. Traditional assessment methods involve open-ended tasks; these produce unpredictable student responses which only a tutor can mark and which take considerable time to read and judge. Marking of this kind takes experience and expertise and cannot be mechanised.

Open-ended tasks are used, in many subject areas, to assess all course objectives. However, a proportion of course objectives are concerned with factual knowledge, the routine application of procedures or calculations, and these objectives can easily be tested more quickly and cheaply. It is not proposed that mechanised assessment can replace conventional assessment procedures entirely, but that some assessment purposes can be achieved in this way, leaving tutors to concentrate on what only they can do.

Two forms of mechanised assessment are considered here:

3.5.1 Objective tests and computer marking
3.5.2 Assignment attachment sheets

3.5.1   Objective tests and computer marking

Objective tests are simply tests which produce student answers (or responses, or actions, or products) that can be marked objectively. There are a number of potential advantages of objective tests in the context of large classes.

*   They can be marked quickly. This is especially the case when students indicate their answers by ticking possible alternatives, as with multiple choice questions.

*   They can be highly reliable. This is important where a team of tutors are involved to cope with a huge assessment load.

- They can be marked easily. This can allow less experienced tutors (for example, postgraduates or third-year undergraduates), students' peers or even computers to mark student work.

The main disadvantages of objective tests are that they are often used to test only superficial learning outcomes involving factual knowledge, and that they do not provide students with feedback. However, it is possible to devise objective tests which involve analysis, computation, interpretation and understanding and yet which are still easily marked. And students knowing how they have done on a multiple choice question test can provide more feedback than is otherwise available in large classes. It is also possible to provide computerised tutorial feedback for students when they give incorrect answers to multiple choice questions.

Objective tests can be used in a variety of ways with large classes:

- To provide regular feedback to students on their progress. They can then use this information in making decisions about what further work they need to do or about whether to attend additional classes. Used as a self-diagnostic tool in this way they enable courses with large enrolments to offer remedial and specialist help only to those who need it, so keeping numbers down. (For an example of a course design in which tests are used in this way see Booklet 1: *Problems and Course Design Strategies*.)

- To replace more time-consuming forms of assessment. Objective tests are particularly useful as one component of assessment, achieving some of the assessment system's aims very economically so that more resources can be allocated to other more demanding forms of assessment.

- To provide tutors with information on the progress of the whole class and help them to make decisions about, for example, the content of remedial lectures or problem sessions.

- To focus students' attention on some basic features of the content of the course, which, in the absence of tutorials, might otherwise slip past.

- As alternatives to conventional exams, or at least the short-answer first sections of conventional exams.

The main forms of objective test questions are:

right/wrong	multiple choice
short answer	multiple completion
completion	assertion/reason
true/false	best answer
matching	

(Fuller explanations of these forms of question, with illustrative examples, may be found in Gibbs *et al.*, 1987.) Examples of six types of question are illustrated in the following extract from *Teaching Geography in Higher Education* (Gold *et al*, 1991).

Types of Objective Test

Short answer

Q. Name three of the "first generartion" New Towns that were designated in Great Britain between 1946 and 1950:

1 ....

2 ....

3 ....

Completion

Q. Central Place Theory was originally formulated by .... in Germany in the 1930s.

True/False

1 Modern crofting was founded by the 1886 Crofters' Holdings Act.   TRUE / FALSE

2 The run-rig system was introduced by Jethro Tull.   TRUE / FALSE

3 Kelping was widely practised in the interior parts of
   Highland Scotland.   TRUE / FALSE

Matching

Q. Match each of the writers in List Y with one of the books in List X by filling in the boxes below the lists. Do not use any of the boxes more than once.

List X		List Y	
1	*Towards a New Architecture*	A	Herman Muthesius
2	*Yesterday: A Peaceful Path to Real Reform*	B	Lewis Mumford
3	*When Democracy Builds*	C	Patrick Geddes
4	*The Culture of Cities*	D	Frank Lloyd Wright
5	*The English House*	E	Ebenezer Howard
		F	Walter Gropius
		G	Le Corbusier

List X   1   2   3   4   5

List Y   ☐   ☐   ☐   ☐   ☐

Multiple Choice

Q. In a test with a mean of 100 and a standard deviation of 12, a raw score of 124 is equal to a standard score of:

A +24

B -2

C +2

D 84%

E 124%

Best Answer

Q. What does the term "teleological" mean when applied to the early attempts of geographers to study the relationship between people and of the environment?

1 the view that the earth has been designed for human purposes by a supreme being

2 the argument that human beings are an integral part of their environment

3 that people are at the mercy of their physical environment

4 that people should always seek to change their environment to suit their own ends

5 that the environment never changes

A common criticism of such objective tests is that they test only very low-level objectives and that they are therefore suitable only for certain kinds of subject matter and perhaps certain disciplines. While it is true that it is easier to test low-level objectives in this way, it is perfectly possible to set very challenging multiple choice questions. In the example below, questions 1-3 cannot be answered unless students have understood the meaning of the terms involved and have some experience of using the terms to categorise qualitative data. Question 4 cannot be answered without an understanding of the terminology and an ability to interpret data. Limits to the appropriate use of objective tests lie only in the imagination of lecturers.

Questions 1-3

Read the following statement by a student:
"I find it difficult to concentrate when I'm reading. I try but it just doesn't seem to go in. When I've got to the end sometimes I haven't learnt much of it. I can go over it several times but nothing much seems to go in. I suppose for some people they can just pass their eyes over a book and they've learnt it all. Afterwards they can simply write it all down. Not me! When I came here I didn't really know what to expect. It was just what everyone thought I would do after school and I just went along with them."

1   What APPROACH to learning does this student describe?
   A   deep approach
   B   unclear - could be deep, could be surface
   C   surface approach

2   What CONCEPTION OF LEARNING does this student seem to have?
   A   learning as an increase in knowledge
   B   learning as memorisation
   C   learning as acquiring facts or procedures for later use
   D   learning as understanding
   E   learning as making sense of reality

3   What ORIENTATION does this student reveal ?
   A   vocational extrinsic
   B   academic intrinsic
   C   academic extrinsic
   D   personal extrinsic
   E   social

Question 4

Consider this data (from Marton and Säljo, 1976) which shows what happened when 30 students read an article and were then interviewed about what they had understood, and about how they had gone about their reading.

Level of learning outcome *	Level of approach		
	Surface	Not clear	Deep
A	0	0	5
B	1	6	4
C	8	0	0
D	5	1	0

* A = full understanding, D = least full understanding.

Consider the following interpretations of the above data:
I   Students who took a deep approach gained a full understanding.
II   Students who took a surface approach did not gain a full understanding.
III Students who took a surface approach did not gain any understanding.
IV   The understanding students gained was related to their approach.
V   The understanding students gained was caused by their approach.

Which of the above statements are true ?
A   I and II
B   II and IV
C   III and IV
D   I and IV
E   II and V

Formulating effective objective tests can be difficult and time-consuming if you have never done it before. However, there are published compendiums of ready-made questions. Many of the large American publishers, particularly those publishing key texts for large introductory courses, also sell compendiums of multiple choice questions, which can either be used as supplied, or modified; they can even be given to students for self-testing. This can obviously save a considerable amount of time.

All the forms of objective tests which require students simply to tick boxes can be computer-marked. Normally this involves the use of standard answer forms which can be read automatically by an optical mark reader, the data from which are fed into a database in a microcomputer. Hardware and software can cost very little and can be easy for a non-specialist to use. Probably the ideal arrangement is for the institution's computer centre to set up a multiple choice test- marking system as a data preparation service (see Gibbs, 1989).

There are also cheap software packages which enable you to present questions on a micro computer screen. Students log in and the answers are recorded and marks collated automatically. Some systems also allow you to type in remedial tutorial comments attached to each incorrect answer, so that when a student finishes a test the print-out contains not only a set of marks but also comments on why the incorrectly answered questions were incorrect.

References

Gibbs, G. (1989), *Using the Optical Mark Reader,* 2: *Collating Multiple Choice Question Test Scores.* Oxford: Educational Methods Unit, Oxford Polytechnic

Gibbs, G., Habeshaw, S. and Habeshaw, T. (1989), *53 Interesting Ways to Assess your Students.* Bristol: Technical and Educational Services

Gibbs, G., Habeshaw, S. and Habeshaw, T. (1992), *53 Interesting Ways to Teach Large Classes.* Bristol: Technical and Educational Services

Gold, J., Jenkins, A. , Lee, R., Monk, J., Riley, J., Shepherd, I. and Unwin, D. (1991), *Teaching Geography in Higher Education.* Oxford: Basil Blackwell

3.5.2   Assignment attachment sheets

Assignment attachment sheets enable tutors to give students feedback quickly by simply ticking boxes to indicate how well the students did in relation to set criteria, or to indicate what feedback statement is appropriate. Students appreciate such forms because they are clear and easy to interpret and because feedback is explicitly related to criteria. Students can see at a glance where their marks came from. Four examples are offered:

1   Criteria which could be used for many types of report writing (from an Energy and Life Systems course at Murdoch University, Australia).

2   A Psychology Practical Comment Sheet. This type of system can be computerised using an optical mark reader (see 3.5.1 "Objective tests and computer marking") to print out a full written report for each student. This kind of computer-based tutorial comment system is used extensively in schools for writing reports on pupils and should not be beyond the resources and competence of academics to use in higher education.

3   Criteria for students assessing a poster session (see also 3.2: "Doing it in class ").

4   A laboratory marking sheet. This also employs a method of briefing students under each heading (see 3.1: "Front-ending assessment").

In addition the self-assessment sheet for English essays above (see 3.3: "Self- and peer-assessment") can be used by tutors to provide feedback and marks.

Assignment attachment sheets can be especially useful where part-time or other tutors are brought in to help with marking and need to be given clear guidelines. It is usually more acceptable for such forms to be used to structure commenting but to leave the award of an overall mark or grade up to the independent judgement of the tutor. Where rating scales are used to award marks, the range and distribution of marks obtained can be different from that achieved through global subjective judgements, and the overall worth of a piece of work is likely to be more than the sum of its parts.

Report Assignment Attachment Form

Energy and Life Systems assignment attachment
(Prepared by Educational Services and Teaching Resources, Murdoch University)

Students' Name
Assignment Grade

Lines left blank by the tutor
are not relevant to this assignment

Key to Grades
A   Outstanding in all respects
B   Some very good features
C   Satisfactory overall
D   Some serious inadequacies
F   Inadequate in most respects

Structure

Essay relevant to topic   ☐☐☐☐☐ Essay has little relevance

Topic covered in depth   ☐☐☐☐☐ Superficial treatment of topic

Argument

Accurate presentation   ☐☐☐☐☐ Much evidence inaccurate
of evidence   or questionable

Logically developed   ☐☐☐☐☐ Essay rambles and lacks
argument   continuity

Originality

Original and creative thought ☐☐☐☐☐ Little evidence of originality

Style

Fluent piece of writing   ☐☐☐☐☐ Clumsily written

Succinct writing   ☐☐☐☐☐ Unnecessarily repetitive

Presentation

Legible and well set out   ☐☐☐☐☐ Untidy and difficult to read

Reasonable length   ☐☐☐☐☐ Under/over length

Sources

Adequate acknowledgement ☐☐☐☐☐ Some plagiarism
of sources

Correct citation of references ☐☐☐☐☐ Incorrect referencing

Mechanics

Sentences grammatical   ☐☐☐☐☐ Several ungrammatical sentences

Correct spelling throughout ☐☐☐☐☐ Much incorrect spelling

Effective use of figures   ☐☐☐☐☐ Figures and tables add little
and tables   to argument

Correct use of units   ☐☐☐☐☐ Some units incorrect
and quantities

Explanation and other comments

Tutor _____

Psychology Practical Comment Sheet

Name: ....   Date Submitted: ....

Practical: ....   Mark: ....

Marker: ....

Checklist of Comments

TITLE
( ) Missing ( ) Correct ( ) Incorrect ( ) Vague   ( ) Too short   ( ) Too long
( ) Incorrect but adequate

ABSTRACT
( ) Needs the heading "Abstract" or "Summary" ( ) Section missing ( ) Too short
( ) Too long (max. 200 words) ( ) Unclear
( ) Wrongly placed, it should be at the beginning
( ) Omits hypothesis/aim - design procedure results - conclusion
( ) Material which is here belongs elsewhere, e.g.
( ) Clear ( ) Succinct

INTRODUCTION
( ) Section missing ( ) Heading missing
( ) Too short (min. 300 w) ( ) About right length ( ) Too long (max. 1,000 w)
( ) Follows handout too closely ( ) Rambling and unfocussed
( ) Does not incorporate a statement of the hypothesis
( ) Rationale for study missing
( ) Does not review previous empirical findings ( ) Omits relevant readings
( ) Does not consider appropriate theories
( ) Some material included here belongs elsewhere, e.g.
( ) Inappropriate use of references   ( ) Well argued
( ) Shows set reading has been done

METHOD
( ) The entire section is missing   ( ) Should be sub-divided as below:

Subjects
( ) Number? ( ) Groups? ( ) Sex? ( ) Age? ( ) Naive to purposes of study

Materials/Apparatus
( ) Section missing   ( ) Not enough detail   ( ) Too much detail
( ) Needs diagram

Design
( ) Section missing   ( ) Control(s)? ( ) Balancing? ( ) Randomisation?

Procedure
( ) Section missing   ( ) Instructions to subjects? ( ) Details missing
( ) Too detailed   ( ) Whole section clear and detailed

Results
Tables
( ) Missing   ( ) Summary table needed
( ) Calculations/Raw data go in Appendix
( ) No numbers/titles on tables (e.g. "Table 1: Mean errors for each age group")
( ) Untidy ( ) Neat

Figures/Graphs
( ) Missing   ( ) Axes need labelling   ( ) Key to symbols? ( ) Wrong items plotted
( ) Bad scaling on axes   ( ) No numbers/titles on figures (e.g. "Figure 1: Graph of")
( ) Untidy   ( ) Neat
Description of Data
( ) Missing   ( ) Too short   ( ) Good length   ( ) Put some of this in Discussion
Statistics
( ) You have not done all the tests described in class
( ) Link this with a table/result.
( ) Arithmetic errors   ( ) Tables/figures neat and well presented
( ) Verbal description clear/precise

DISCUSSION
( ) Missing   ( ) Little evidence that you have done the required reading
( ) Too short   ( ) Too long
( ) Mention problems with procedure/design
( ) Does not pick up points raised in the Introduction
( ) Conclusion missing   ( ) Your conclusion is not justified from the data presented
( ) Material has been included here which would go better in the Introduction
( ) Satisfactory   ( ) Well organised   ( ) Well organised and well argued
( ) Contains some novel and interesting opinions

REFERENCES
( ) Some references are incomplete
Minimum information is :
(a) first author   (b) title of article or book   (c) title of journal (if relevant)
(d) volume number   (e) year of publication   (f) publisher (books only)
( ) Some references made in report are not detailed here
( ) Some references are inaccurate
( ) Section missing   ( ) Satisfactory

GENERAL
( ) Poor   ( ) Fair   ( ) Good   ( ) Very good   ( ) Excellent
( ) Too brief overall   ( ) Too hurriedly written
( ) Report not set out in formal order
( ) Poor spelling   ( ) Poor grammar   ( ) Untidy
( ) Difficult to follow your arguments: muddled, disorganised
( ) Too long (you need to demonstrate skill in condensing your argument)
( ) Overall presentation above average
( ) Demonstrates reading beyond set references and extra marks have been
   awarded for this

This sheet is one of a series prepared by the Psychology Unit, Oxford Polytechnic, and is reproduced here with the permission of Dr R. Paton.

Poster Assessment Criteria

		4	3	2	1	0	
1	Self-explanatory	☐	☐	☐	☐	☐	Requires extensive additional information to be understood

Comments:

		4	3	2	1	0	
2	Clear purpose (or hypothesis)	☐	☐	☐	☐	☐	Unclear purpose (or no hypothesis)

Comments:

		4	3	2	1	0	
3	Clear and appropriate methodology	☐	☐	☐	☐	☐	Unclear/inappropriate methodology

Comments:

		4	3	2	1	0	
4	Clear and justified conclusion	☐	☐	☐	☐	☐	Unclear/unjustified conclusion

Comments:

		4	3	2	1	0	
5	Clear theoretical basis/implications	☐	☐	☐	☐	☐	Unclear theoretical basis/implications

Comments:

Total score (out of 20):

Other criteria could include:

Visually effective and attractive ⟵⟶ Visually ineffective and unattractive

Helpful level of detail ⟵⟶ Unhelpful/inappropriate level of detail

Means of data analysis and interpretation clear and appropriate ⟵⟶ Means of data analysis and interpretation unclear/inappropriate

Laboratory Report Briefing and Assessment Sheet

Lab briefing and assessment sheet

Lab..

Student...

Section	Briefing	Max mark	Your mark	Feedback
Introduction Background				
Methodology Use of equipment				
Results Data analysis				
Discussion Conclusion				

References

Gibbs, G. and Jaques, D. (1990), *Labs and Practicals.* Oxford: Educational Methods Unit, Oxford Polytechnic.

MacDonald, R. and Sanson, D. (1979), "Use of Assignment Attachments in Assessment", *Assessment in Higher Education*, 5 (1), 45-55.

3.6 Cutting down on assessment and feedback

If this strategy involved only cutting down on assessment and feedback it would have the negative consequences identified at the start of this booklet. To avoid these problems, cutting down has to be strategic. It has to concentrate time and effort on those aspects of assessment which have the most positive impact on student learning, and reluctantly let go of some other aspects of assessment.

3.6.1 Cutting down on assessment

3.6.2 Cutting down on feedback

3.6.3 Using the assessment regulations to help

3.6.1 Cutting down on assessment

The obvious step to take to cope with excessive marking loads is to cut down on the total amout of assessment. However, simply reducing the number of essays, labs or problem sheets may be the best way to guarantee lower-quality learning. Cutting down should be a strategic move with specific goals in mind, letting go of some things in order to hold on to others that you care about. For example:

- Distinguish between assessment which leads to learning and assessment which merely samples what students have learnt for the purposes of awarding marks. You may be able to adopt quite different strategies for these two elements: finding ways to give less, but more focussed, feedback (see below) and ways to obtain reliable marks in less time (as described in 3.5: "Mechanising assessment").

- Use more varied assessment methods. Essays may be appropriate for some educational goals but are a very expensive way to allocate marks. A mixture of fewer essays backed up by objective tests might ensure both development of writing and reasoning skills and broad coverage of material.

- Cut out repetitive assessment. It is not clear that writing laboratory reports every week is necessary for students either to learn from the laboratory work or to develop writing skills. Indeed, some such assignments have become so repetitive that they serve few useful functions.

- Distinguish between courses with different goals. Some courses have aims which may be best assessed through short tests rather than long essays or reports. Accept that different courses should have unique assessment patterns rather than all courses being assessed with the same type and volume of assignments.

- Cut down on the length of exams. Unless you have evidence that three-hour exams are necessary, experiment with two- or even one-hour exams.

3.6.2 Cutting down on feedback

A number of ideas for strategically focussing feedback, and so reducing it, have been outlined in the sections above. Specific examples of this broad strategy include:

- Only give full comments when students are relatively certain to read and respond to them, for example, when you are commenting on the drafts of research reports. Try to avoid detailed marking of extensive pieces of work when students are unlikely to want to, or are even not allowed to, see your marking.

- Concentrate feedback on early stages of assignments at a point when it can have an impact on learning through re-drafting, rather than on finished products. It may be possible simply to award a mark to the final product, perhaps with a proportion of these marks allocated to the extent to which the students responded to feedback on the draft.

- Ask students what they want feedback on. They could write a request on their assignment or on a self-assessment sheet. You can even offer them a check-list and ask them to identify three main areas for comments. Students should be made aware of your limited time and made to think about how they want to use it most productively.

- Devise fewer but bigger assignments. This might involve portfolios of work collected over the year or a complete lab notebook containing all the laboratory reports for the year. The fewer the number of occasions on which you mark, the less time it is likely to take you overall, even if the portfolio itself is time-consuming to assess.

- Use students themselves to provide feedback wherever possible (see 3.3: "Self- and peer-assessment").

- Instead of providing detailed comments on everyone's work, write a summary of issues raised by everyone's work and distribute this, together with a mark for each student.

- Use feedback forms to structure and limit feedback (see 3. 5: "Mechanising assessment").

- Use briefings to focus students' attention on only a few aspects of an assignment each time (for example, on only measurement and accuracy in a lab report) and give feedback only on these few aspects (see 3. 1: "Front-ending assessment").

- Use audio-tape to comment on students' work. This is not likely to cut down on feedback but it can save a lot of time. As you read, speak your comments into a tape recorder. Do not write any down but just indicate by numbers on the text (1,2,3...) to which specific sections your comments refer. Students frequently say that they get far more information from taped comments, including the tone of one's voice, than they do from written comments, and they also do not have to try to cope with some of our illegible writing.

  It may be important to ensure that tape recorders (and tapes) are available in the department/institution so that students can listen to your comments. However, if you use the audio-tapes that fit into a Walkman/conventional cassette tape recorder, you may find this is not necessary, as students have their own machines.

Students can be required to hand in a blank tape with their assignment, and to have listened carefully to your tape-recorded comments before they have any tutorial time with you to discuss their work. If they have not, refuse to see them. They soon get the message. This ensures that your expensive time is used to maximum effect. It has been known for students to tape these discussions as well.

Reference

Cryer, P. and Kaikumba, N. (1987), Audio-Cassette Tape as a Means of Giving Feedback on Written Work, *Assessment and Evaluation in Higher Education*, 12 (2), 148-153.

3.6.3 Using the assessment regulations to help

Exam and assessment regulations have not always been designed to help cope with large student numbers, and a review of some of these regulations may be overdue. For example, you can:

- Set clear deadlines for work and do not allow late submission to extend the period you have set aside for marking.

- Require all work to be handed in to secretaries or technicians and insist that it be checked off when handed in. Keep as far away from the administration of handling assessed work as possible.

- Require all work to be typed, or word-processed and printed. Departmental investment in computers can repay itself in saved marking time.

- Refuse to accept illegible work.

NOTE
The last two suggestions will need monitoring to check that students with genuine disabilities are not unfairly penalised.

- Set strict word or page limits to assignments and simply refuse to read material beyond these limits. It is in any case good practice for students to work to word limits: most people both outside and within academia have to keep to word limits all the time.

- Ensure that regulations devised for an earlier time (e.g. there should be two three-hour unseen exams; all work should be double-marked; essays should be 5,000 words) are not allowed to lead to inappropriate and unworkable assessment arrangements.

- Streamline arrangements for re-sits, which often do not need to be as elaborate as the first assessment.

- Review the necessity for extensive assessment in the first year, where most assessment is pass/fail (in the sense of decisions concerning progression to the second year, rather than marks counting towards the final degree) and where almost all students pass regardless of the assessment system used.

Bibliography

Andresen, L., Nightingale, P., Boud, D. and Magin, D. (1989), Strategies for Assessing Students, Teaching with Reduced Resources, no. 1. Kensington: Professional Development Centre, University of New South Wales

Boud, D. (1986), Implementing Student Self-Assessment, Green Guide no. 5. Sydney: Higher Education Research and Development Society of Australasia

Cox, K. R. and Ewan, C. E. (1988), The Medical Teacher. Edinburgh: Churchill Livingstone (especially the following chapters: "Writing mulitple choice questions", "How to construct a fair multiple choice question-paper", "How to organise multiple choice question banks", "What teachers and students get out of multiple choice examinations")

Gibbs, G. ed. (1985), Alternatives in Assessment 2: Objective Tests and Computer Applications. Standing Conference on Educational Development, Paper no. 21. Birmingham: Standing Conference on Educational Development

Gibbs, G., Habeshaw, S. and Habeshaw, T. (1992), 53 Interesting Ways To Teach Large Classes. Bristol: Technical and Educational Services

Gibbs, G., Habeshaw, S. and Habeshaw, T. (1989), 53 Interesting Ways To Assess Your Students. Bristol: Technical and Educational Services

Lowman, J. (1987), "Giving students feedback" in M. G. Weimer (ed.) Teaching Large Classes Well. London: Jossey-Bass

MacDonald, R. and Sansom, D. (1979), "Use of Assignment Attachments in Assessment," Assesment in Higher Education, 5 (1), 45-55.

Rowntree, D. (1987), Assessing students: how shall we know them? London: Kogan Page

Wolford, G. L. (1975), "Assessment of student performance," in G. L. Wolford and W. M. Smith (eds.), Large Course Instruction. Hanover, New Hampshire: Dartmouth College